First World War
and Army of Occupation
War Diary
France, Belgium and Germany

27 DIVISION
81 Infantry Brigade
Royal Scots (Lothian Regiment)
9th Battalion
26 February 1915 - 31 December 1915

WO95/2264/2

The Naval & Military Press Ltd
www.nmarchive.com
Published in association with The National Archives

Published by

The Naval & Military Press Ltd

Unit 10 Ridgewood Industrial Park,

Uckfield, East Sussex,

TN22 5QE England

Tel: +44 (0) 1825 749494

www.naval-military-press.com

www.nmarchive.com

This diary has been reprinted in facsimile from the original. Any imperfections are inevitably reproduced and the quality may fall short of modern type and cartographic standards.

© Crown Copyright
Images reproduced by permission of The National Archives, London, England, 2015.

Contents

Document type	Place/Title	Date From	Date To
Heading	WO95/2264/2		
Heading	27th Division 81st Infy Bde 9th Bn Royal Scots 1915 Feb-1915 Dec To 51 Bn 154 Bde		
Heading	81st Inf. Bde. 27th Div. Battn. Disembarked Havre 26.2.15 War Diary 9th Battn. The Royal Scots. 26th February To 31st March 1915		
War Diary	Havre	26/02/1915	27/02/1915
War Diary	Cassel	28/02/1915	28/02/1915
War Diary	L'Abeele	01/03/1915	07/03/1915
War Diary	Dickebusch	07/03/1915	07/03/1915
War Diary	L'Abeele	08/03/1915	08/03/1915
War Diary	Dickebusch	08/03/1915	08/03/1915
War Diary	L'Abeele	09/03/1915	09/03/1915
War Diary	Dickebusch	09/03/1915	09/03/1915
War Diary	L'Abeele	10/03/1915	10/03/1915
War Diary	Dickebusch	10/03/1915	10/03/1915
War Diary	L'Abeele	11/03/1915	11/03/1915
War Diary	Dickebusch	11/03/1915	11/03/1915
War Diary	L'Abeele	12/03/1915	12/03/1915
War Diary	Dickebusch	12/03/1915	23/03/1915
War Diary	Mt Kokereel	24/03/1915	26/03/1915
War Diary	Ypres	26/03/1915	31/03/1915
Heading	81st Inf. Bde. 27th Div. 9th Battn. The Royal Scots. April 1915		
War Diary	Ypres	01/04/1915	04/04/1915
War Diary	Hooge	05/04/1915	05/04/1915
War Diary	Ypres	05/04/1915	05/04/1915
War Diary	Hooge	06/04/1915	06/04/1915
War Diary	Ypres	06/04/1915	06/04/1915
War Diary	Hooge	07/04/1915	07/04/1915
War Diary	Ypres	07/04/1915	07/04/1915
War Diary	Hooge	08/04/1915	08/04/1915
War Diary	Glencorse Wood	09/04/1915	12/04/1915
War Diary	Vlamertinghe	13/04/1915	15/04/1915
War Diary	Ypres	16/04/1915	16/04/1915
War Diary	Glencorse Wood	17/04/1915	20/04/1915
War Diary	Vlamertinghe	21/04/1915	22/04/1915
War Diary	Potijze	23/04/1915	23/04/1915
War Diary	Weiltje	23/04/1915	23/04/1915
War Diary	St.Julien	23/04/1915	23/04/1915
War Diary	Weiltje	23/04/1915	23/04/1915
War Diary	St Jean	23/04/1915	27/04/1915
War Diary	Sanctuary Wood	28/04/1915	30/04/1915
Heading	81st Inf. Bde. 27th Div. War Diary 9th Battn. The Royal Scots. May 1915		
War Diary	Hooge	01/05/1915	22/05/1915
War Diary	Busseboom	23/05/1915	24/05/1915
War Diary	Vlamertinghe	25/05/1915	25/05/1915
War Diary	Busse Boom	26/05/1915	28/05/1915
War Diary	Dranoutre	29/05/1915	29/05/1915

War Diary	Steenwerck	30/05/1915	30/05/1915
War Diary	Armentieres	31/05/1915	31/05/1915
Heading	81st Inf. Bde. 27th Div. War Diary 9th Battn. The Royal Scots. June 1915		
War Diary	Armentieres	01/06/1915	07/06/1915
War Diary	Chapelle D'Armentieres	08/06/1915	30/06/1915
Heading	81st Inf. Bde. 27th Div. War Diary 9th Battn. The Royal Scots. July 1915		
War Diary	Orchard Rue Gattignies	01/07/1915	31/07/1915
Heading	81st Inf. Bde. 27th Div. War Diary 9th Battn. The Royal Scots. August 1915		
War Diary	The Orchard Rue Gattignies	01/08/1915	02/08/1915
War Diary	Erquinghem	03/08/1915	16/08/1915
War Diary	La Vesee	16/08/1915	31/08/1915
Heading	81st Inf. Bde. 27th Div. War Diary 9th Battn. The Royal Scots. September 1915		
War Diary	La Vesee	01/09/1915	15/09/1915
War Diary	Erquinghem	16/09/1915	17/09/1915
War Diary	Vieux Berquin	18/09/1915	20/09/1915
War Diary	Lamotte En Santerre	21/09/1915	30/09/1915
Heading	81st Inf. Bde. 27th Div. War Diary 9th Battn. The Royal Scots. October 1915		
War Diary	Lamotte En Santerre	01/10/1915	03/10/1915
War Diary	Fontaine Les Cappy	04/10/1915	24/10/1915
War Diary	Lamotte En Santerre	25/10/1915	26/10/1915
War Diary	Boves	27/10/1915	27/10/1915
War Diary	Bougainville	28/10/1915	31/10/1915
Heading	81st Bde. 27th Div. War Diary Left To Join 5th Division 24th Nov. 1915 9th Royal Scots November 1915		
War Diary	Bougainville	01/11/1915	23/11/1915
War Diary	Ferrieres	24/11/1915	24/11/1915
War Diary	Pont Noyelles	25/11/1915	25/11/1915
War Diary	Sailly Lorette	26/11/1915	26/11/1915
War Diary	Suzanne	27/11/1915	28/11/1915
War Diary	Vaux	27/11/1915	28/11/1915
War Diary	Suzanne	29/11/1915	29/11/1915
War Diary	Vaux	30/11/1915	30/11/1915
Heading	9/R. Scots Intell Report Nov 1915		
War Diary	Vaux	29/11/1915	30/11/1915
Heading	5th Division 14th Bde 9th Royal Scots Come From 27 Div. Nov 24-15 December 1915		
Heading	14th Bde. 5th Div. Came From 27th Division 24th November 1915 9th Royal Scots December 1915		
War Diary	Vaux	01/12/1915	31/12/1915

W095/2264/2

27TH DIVISION
81ST INFY BDE

9TH BN ROYAL SCOTS

~~FEB - NOV 1915~~
1915 FEB — 1915 DEC

To 51 DN · 154 BDE

81st Inf.Bde.
27th Div.

Battn. disembarked
Havre 26.2.15.

WAR DIARY

9th BATTN. THE ROYAL SCOTS.

26TH FEBRUARY TO 31ST MARCH 1915.

WAR DIARY

or

INTELLIGENCE SUMMARY.

(Erase heading not required.)

Place	Date	Hour	Summary of Events and Information	Remarks and references to Appendices
HAVRE	26/2/15	—	The Battalion, strength 30 Officers & 987 other Ranks arrived at HAVRE on board H.M.T. INVENTOR. at 6.30 a.m. & commenced disembarking at 7. a.m. Disembarkation completed by 11. a.m. Two platoons of A Coy under command of Capt. P.A. Blair were ordered to entrain at 1.30 p.m. destination L'ABEELE. The remainder of the Battalion marched to No 1 Rest Camp HAVRE (4 miles) & spent the night 26th 27th February there.	H.M.D. Capt & Adjt
HAVRE	27/2/15	—	The Battalion less 2 platoons of A Coy paraded at 7.30. a.m. and marched to LA GARE DES MERCHANDISES HAVRE (3½ miles) & commenced entraining at 9. a.m. Entraining was completed by 11. a.m. the train started at 12.50 p.m. Destination L'ABEELE	P.M.D. Capt & Adjt
CASSEL	28/2/15	—	The Train arrived at CASSEL at 10. a.m. Detraining was completed by 11 a.m. it had been arranged for the men & the battalion moved off at 12.30 p.m. & marched to L'ABEELE Station (12 miles) arriving there at 5 p.m. The Two Platoons of A Coy under Capt. P.A. Blair rejoined the Battalion there. The battalion was billeted in farm buildings in the neighbourhood of L'ABEELE Station	R.M.D. Capt & Adjt

WAR DIARY
or
INTELLIGENCE SUMMARY.

(Erase heading not required.)

Instructions regarding War Diaries and Intelligence Summaries are contained in F.S. Regs., Part II. and the Staff Manual respectively. Title pages will be prepared in manuscript.

Place	Date	Hour	Summary of Events and Information	Remarks and references to Appendices
L'ABEELE	1/3/15	—	The battalion was employed in working on the improvement of their billets. Lieut N.H. Young 1/10" Royal Scots Fus.[attached to the battalion] for instructional purposes.	P.h.D. Capt & Adjt
L'ABEELE	2/3/15	—	A Coy paraded in their billets at 9.30 a.m. to a lecture on Trench Warfare by Lieut N.H. Young and at 6.30 p.m. for instruction in the method of moving up to & taking over trenches by night. The remainder of the battalion were employed in making fascines from 9.30 a.m. to 4.30 p.m. with an hours interval for dinner.	P.h.D. Capt & Adjt
L'ABEELE	3/3/15	—	The battalion paraded at 10 a.m. for inspection by Brigadier General MacFarlane Commanding 81st Infy Brigade. B Coy paraded in their billets a 2 p.m. to a lecture on Trench Warfare by Lieut N.H. Young & at 7 p.m. for instruction in moving up to & taking over trenches by night. The remainder of the battalion were employed in making fascines from 2 p.m. to 4.30 p.m.	P.h.D. Capt & Adjt

INTELLIGENCE SUMMARY

(Erase heading not required.)

Instructions regarding War Diaries and Intelligence Summaries are contained in F.S. Regs., Part II. and the Staff Manual respectively. Title pages will be prepared in manuscript.

Place	Date	Hour	Summary of Events and Information	Remarks and references to Appendices
L'ABEELE	4/3/15	—	Lieut L.W. Young [Von Royals Scots] left [at 9 a.m.] to rejoin his battalion. The battalion was employed in making fascines from 9.30 a.m. to 4.30 p.m. with an hour interval for dinner. In the evening Coys paraded at 7 p.m. + practised moving up to + taking over trenches.	R.W.D. Capt 1 Adjt.
L'ABEELE	5/3/15	—	[Same as 4/3/15.] 2nd Lieut R Thompson admitted to hospital [at BOESCHEPE].	R.W.D. Capt 1 Adjt.
L'ABEELE	6/3/15	—	A C + D Coys employed in making fascines from 9.30 a.m. to 4.30 P.M. + in the evening paraded at 7 p.m. + practised moving up to + taking over trenches. B. Coy paraded at 12.30 p.m. + marched to DICKEBUSCH (12 miles) arriving there at 5 p.m. Two platoons under Capt J. Ferguson were employed in/building up barbed wire entanglements + marking trenches near VOORMEZEELE until carried on till 4 a.m. 7th March. Lieut Col A.S. Blair [was admitted] to hospital [at BAILLEUL].	R.W.D. Capt 1 Adjt.

INTELLIGENCE SUMMARY

(Erase heading not required.)

Instructions regarding War Diaries and Intelligence Summaries are contained in F. S. Regs., Part II. and the Staff Manual respectively. Title pages will be prepared in manuscript.

Place	Date	Hour	Summary of Events and Information	Remarks and references to Appendices
L'ABEELE	7/3/15	—	A C & D Coys were employed in making fascines [from 9.30 a.m. to 4.30 P.M.] + in the evening [Keys paraders at 7 p.m.] + practical training in patrols & lobbing over trenches	W.h.D. Capt & adjt.
DICKEBUSCH	7/3/15	—	B Coy [were employed in planting up wire entanglements + revetting trenches near VOORMEZEELE [from 8 p.m. till 4 a.m. 8/3/15]	R.h.D. Capt & adjt.
L'ABEELE	8/3/15	—	A. C. & D Coys Same as 7/3/15.	R.h.D. Capt & adjt.
DICKEBUSCH	8/3/15	—	B Coy Same as 7/3/15.	R.h.D. Capt & adjt.
L'ABEELE	9/3/15	—	A C & D Coys Same as 7/3/15.	R.h.D. Capt & adjt.
DICKEBUSCH	9/3/15	—	B Coy were employed in digging trenches near VIERSTRAAT from 8 p.m. till 1 a.m. 10/3/15.	R.h.D. Capt & adjt.
L'ABEELE	10/3/15	—	C & D Coys Same as 7/3/15.	R.h.D. Capt & adjt.

1577 Wt.W10791/1773 500,000 1/15 D. D. & L. A.D.S.S./Forms/C. 2118.

INTELLIGENCE SUMMARY.

(Erase heading not required.)

Instructions regarding War Diaries and Intelligence Summaries are contained in F. S. Regs., Part II. and the Staff Manual respectively. Title pages will be prepared in manuscript.

Place	Date	Hour	Summary of Events and Information	Remarks and references to Appendices
L'ABEELE	10/3/15	—	A Coy paraded at 12.30 p.m. & marched to DICKEBUSCH (1½ miles) arriving there 5 p.m.	R.L.S. Coppard
L'ABEELE	10/3/15	—	C & D Coys were employed in making fascines from 9.30 a.m. to 4.30 p.m. and at 7 p.m. paraded for instruction in traversing, repairs & taking over trenches.	R.L.S. Coppard
DICKEBUSCH	10/3/15	—	B. Coy were employed in digging trenches between VIERSTRAAT & the BRASSERIE from 8 p.m. to 12 M.N. No 1773 W.C. McMillan wounded	R.L.S. Coppard
L'ABEELE	11/3/15	—	C & D Coys Same as 10/3/15	
DICKEBUSCH	11/3/15	—	A Coy employed in cleaning up DICKEBUSCH HUT SHELTERS. B. Coy Two platoons paraded at 6 p.m. under Capt. J. Ferguson, as a Carrying party returning at 11.45 p.m. No 2003 Pte A Bishop wounded. Two platoons under Capt D.Bell digging trenches between BRASSERIE & VIERSTRAAT from 8 p.m. till 12 M.N.	R.L.S. Coppard

App 5-8

Instructions regarding War Diaries and Intelligence Summaries are contained in F.S. Regs., Part II. and the Staff Manual respectively. Title pages will be prepared in manuscript.

INTELLIGENCE SUMMARY
(Erase heading not required.)

Place	Date	Hour	Summary of Events and Information	Remarks and references to Appendices
L'ABEELE	12/3/15	—	Headquarters & C & D Coys paraded at 12:45 p.m. & marched to DICKEBUSCH (12 miles) Arriving there at 5:30 p.m.	W.D. Capt & adjt
DICKEBUSCH	12/3/15	—	A Coy paraded at 6 p.m. for duty in the Trenches. 2 Platoons attached to 2/Cameron Highlanders and 2 Platoons attached to 1/ L & S. Highlanders No 2190 Pte T. Garry wounded. B. Coy employed in digging trenches between the BRASSERIE and VIERSTRAAT from 10 p.m. till 3 A.M 13/3/15. Lieut Col A.S. Blain rejoined the battalion	W.D. Capt & adjt
DICKEBUSCH	13/3/15	—	A Coy returned from Trenches at 12 M.N. [No 2290] Pte [B.C.O Bealow] wounded. B. Coy employed in digging trenches between the BRASSERIE & VIERSTRAAT from 8 p.m. to 12 M.N. C Coy paraded at 6.30 p.m. for duty in the Trenches, 2 Platoons attached to 1st Royal Scots & 2 Platoons attached to 2/Gloucesters [No 2067 Pte W. Lawson + No 2152 Pte D. Lang wounded.] D Coy employed as carrying parties to trenches from 8 p.m. to 12 M.N	W.D. Capt & adjt

INTELLIGENCE SUMMARY

(Erase heading not required.)

Instructions regarding War Diaries and Intelligence Summaries are contained in F.S. Regs., Part II. and the Staff Manual respectively. Title pages will be prepared in manuscript.

Place	Date	Hour	Summary of Events and Information	Remarks and references to Appendices
DICKEBUSCH	14/3/15	—	A. B. & D Coys standing by. No 14 Platoon (D Coy) carried water & provisions to C Coy in the trenches. No 2164 Pte H C Paterson & No 2475 Pte T H Jack wounded. C Coy in the trenches. [No 27] Sergt [T Crichton] killed & [No 1891] Pte [A. C. Muirhead] wounded.	W.h. & Capt & adjt
DICKEBUSCH	15/3/15	—	A Coy employed in digging trenches from 8 p.m. to 1 a.m. 16/3/15. No 2952 Pte H Gorton & No 2298 Pte R.K. Cormack wounded. B Coy paraded at 6.30 p.m. for duty in the trenches attached to 1st A & S: Highlanders. C Coy returned from the trenches at 11.45 p.m. D Coy paraded at 6.30 p.m. for duty in the trenches attached to 2/Cameron Highlanders.	R.M.O Capt & adjt
DICKEBUSCH	16/3/15	—	A Coy employed in digging trenches from 8 p.m. till 1 a.m. 17/3/15. B Coy returned from trenches at 12. M.N. C Coy resting. D Coy returned from trenches at 12. M.N.	W.h. & Capt & adjt

Instructions regarding War Diaries and Intelligence Summaries are contained in F.S. Regs., Part II. and the Staff Manual respectively. Title pages will be prepared in manuscript.

INTELLIGENCE SUMMARY.

(Erase heading not required.)

Place	Date	Hour	Summary of Events and Information	Remarks and references to Appendices
DICKEBUSCH	17/3/15	—	A. Coy employed in digging trenches from 8 p.m till 1 a.m 18/3/15. B. Coy resting. C. Coy employed as carrying parties from 7 p.m. till 12 M.N. D. Coy resting.	M.O. Capt Ralph
DICKEBUSCH	18/3/15	—	A Coy resting. B.C. & D Coys digging & building parapet on new trench near ST. ELOI in two reliefs each of 300. 1st relief 8 p.m. to 12 M.N. 2nd Relief 12 M.N. to 3.30.a.m 19/3/15. [No 1708 Pte R.A Jamieson & No 1717 Pte J.W. Robertson wounded.]	M.O. Capt Ralph
DICKEBUSCH	19/3/15	—	A B C & D Coys were employed in digging & building parapet on new trench near ST ELOI in two reliefs each of 400 [1st relief 8 p.m. to 12 M.N. 2nd relief 12 M.N. to 3.A.M. 20/3/15. No 2091 Pte W. Blair wounded and No 2181 Pte G.R. Parrott & No 1392 Pte E.G. Barron wounded]	M.O. Capt Ralph
DICKEBUSCH	20/3/15	—	A C & D Coys working on New Trench near ST ELOI in two reliefs each of 300 [1st Relief 8 p.m to 12 M.N 2nd Relief 12 M.N to 3 a.m 21/3/15.] B Coy employed in putting up wire entanglements in front of new Trench near ST.ELOI, in two reliefs each of 60 1st Relief 8 p.m 12 M.N 2nd Relief 12 M.N to 3 a.m 21/3/15. No 1248 Pte J Dryburgh wounded.	M.O. Capt & Adjt

1577 Wt.W10791/1773 500,000 1/15 D. D. & L. A.D.S.S./Forms/C. 2118.

Army Form C. 2118.

INTELLIGENCE SUMMARY.
(Erase heading not required.)

Instructions regarding War Diaries and Intelligence Summaries are contained in F.S. Regs., Part II. and the Staff Manual respectively. Title pages will be prepared in manuscript.

Place	Date	Hour	Summary of Events and Information	Remarks and references to Appendices
DICKEBUSCH	21/3/15	—	A + C Coys working on new Trench near ST ELOI in two reliefs each of 200. 1st Relief 8 p.m. to 12 M.N. 2nd Relief 12 M.N. to 3 a.m. 22/3/15. B Coy employed in putting up wire entanglements in front of new Trench near ST ELOI in two reliefs each of 60. 1st Relief 8 p.m. to 12 M.N. 2nd Relief 12 M.N. to 3 a.m. 22/3/15. D Coy paraded at 6.30 p.m. for duty in Trenches. 1 Platoon attached to 1st Royal Scots + 2 Platoons attached to 2/Gloucesters.	R.M.D. Capts. & Adjt.
DICKEBUSCH	22/3/15	—	A. B + C Coys same as 21/3/15. No 2268 Pte. F.I. Bennet Killed + No 1991 Pte. J. MacDonald + No 1721 Pte. J. Miller wounded, the latter seriously. D Coy still in Trenches	R.M.D. Capts. & Adjt.
DICKEBUSCH	23/3/15	—	Headquarters + A B + C Coys paraded at 8 p.m. + marched to MOUNT KOKEREEL near WESTOUTRE (8½ miles) arriving there at 11.30 p.m. D Coy still in Trenches. No 1436 Pte. R. Stewart wounded.	R.M.D. Capts. & Adjt.

INTELLIGENCE SUMMARY

(Erase heading not required.)

Instructions regarding War Diaries and Intelligence Summaries are contained in F.S. Regs., Part II. and the Staff Manual respectively. Title pages will be prepared in manuscript.

Place	Date	Hour	Summary of Events and Information	Remarks and references to Appendices
Mt ROKEREEL	24/3/15	—	A.B + C. Coys resting. D. Coy relieved from Trenches about 2 a.m. and rejoined the battalion at Mt ROKEREEL at 11.50 a.m.	R.N.D. Capt & Adjt
Mt ROKEREEL	25/3/15	—	Battalion visited in their billets by General Sir H. Plumer Commanding V Corps & Brigadier General H. Croker Commanding 81st Infty Brigade	R.N.D. Capt & Adjt
Mt ROKEREEL	26/3/15	—	Battalion paraded at 7.15 a.m. & marched to YPRES (12 miles) arriving there at 11.50 a.m. & went into billets. A Coy digging trenches 8 p.m. to 12 m.n.	R.N.D. Capt & Adjt
YPRES	27/3/15	—	Coys worked on the improvement of & cleaning up of their billets from 9 a.m. to 4 p.m. B. C. + D. Coys digging trenches from 8 p.m. to 12 m.n. 2 Lieut R Menzies rejoined the battalion from Hospital	R.N.D. Capt Hodge

INTELLIGENCE SUMMARY.

(Erase heading not required.)

Instructions regarding War Diaries and Intelligence Summaries are contained in F. S. Regs., Part II. and the Staff Manual respectively. Title pages will be prepared in manuscript.

Place	Date	Hour	Summary of Events and Information	Remarks and references to Appendices
YPRES	28/3/15	—	C, D & A Coys digging trenches from 12 M N to 3 a.m. 28/3/15. Coy Church parade at 12 NOON	R.W.D. Capt & Adjt
YPRES	29/3/15	—	A, B & D Coys digging trenches from 8 p.m. to 12 M.N.	R.W.D. Capt & Adjt
YPRES	30/3/15	—	A & B Coys digging trenches from 12 M N to 4 a.m. 31/3/15.	R.W.D. Capt & Adjt
YPRES	31/3/15	—	Officers & selected N.C.O's & men paraded at the R E Stores 13 Rue de LOMBARD YPRES, for instruction in the mechanism & throwing of trench bombs, by Lieut. STONNER R.E. A, B, C & D Coys digging trenches from 8 p.m. to 12 M.N.	R.W.D. Capt & Adjt

1577 Wt. W10791/1773 500,000 1/15 D. D. & L. A.D.S.S./Forms/C. 2118.

81st Inf.Bde.
27th Div.

9th BATTN. THE ROYAL SCOTS.

A P R I L

1 9 1 5

Army Form C. 2118.

WAR DIARY

INTELLIGENCE SUMMARY.

9th - Royal Scots.

(Erase heading not required.)

Instructions regarding War Diaries and Intelligence Summaries are contained in F. S. Regs., Part II. and the Staff Manual respectively. Title pages will be prepared in manuscript.

Place	Date	Hour	Summary of Events and Information	Remarks and references to Appendices
YPRES	1915 April 1st		A + B Coys worked on 2nd Line Defences from 12 M.N. to 3.30 a.m. 2/4/15.	W.L.D.
	2nd		C + D Coys ———— do ———— from 8 p.m. to 12 M.N.	W.L.D.
	3rd		A + B Coys ———— do ———— from 12 M.N. to 3.30 a.m. 4/4/15.	W.L.D.
YPRES	4th		H.Q., M.G. Section + A + B Coys move from YPRES to SANCTUARY WOOD, HOOGE to be in close support to the Left Sector of trenches held by 81st Brigade. C + D Coys remain in billets in YPRES.	R.L.D.
HOOGE	5th		Reconnaissance of support trenches by commanding officer, Adjutant + A + B Coy commanders at 11 a.m. A + B Coys worked on support trenches from 8 p.m. to 12 M.N.	R.L.D.
YPRES	"		C + D Coys rest in YPRES.	

R.L. Elwirdson Capt / a.d.f.
9th Royal Scots

WAR DIARY
or
INTELLIGENCE SUMMARY.
(Erase heading not required.)

Army Form C. 2118.

Place	Date	Hour	Summary of Events and Information	Remarks and references to Appendices
HOOGE YPRES	April 6th 6th		A & B Coys worked on support trenches from 8 p.m. to 12 M.N. C & D Coys resting. Capt. Lucas Moncrieff, Lieuts Bennet Clark, Haddow, Richard Macdonald & P.J. Blair visited the Left Sector of trenches of the 81st Brigade held by the 1st A. & S. Highlanders.	R.W.D.
HOOGE YPRES	7th 7th		A & B Coy supplied carrying party for 2nd Cameron Highlanders & 9th A. & S. H. C & D Coys resting. D Coy billets were shelled about 8 a.m. 6 N.C.O's & men were killed and 48 wounded.	R.W.D.
HOOGE	8th		The Battalion moved to GLENCORSE WOOD at 8 p.m. to take over the Left Sector of trenches from the 12th A. & S. Highlanders. C & D Coys & M.G. Section in the trenches. A & B in dugouts in close support.	R.W.D.
GLENCORSE WOOD	9th		C & D Coys & M.G. Section in trenches. A Coy furnished working parties & B Coy carrying parties. No. 2524 Pte. B. Brown A Coy killed & Lieut. P.J. Blair & 10 other ranks wounded. P.W. Hunter, Capt. & Adjt. 9 A. & S. H.	R.W.D.

Army Form C. 2118.

WAR DIARY

or

~~INTELLIGENCE SUMMARY~~

(Erase heading not required.)

III.

Place	Date	Hour	Summary of Events and Information	Remarks and references to Appendices
	April			
GLENCORSE WOOD	10th		A + B Coys relieved C + D Coys in the trenches. No. 1631 Pte J.A. Brass C Coy killed, + 2 other ranks wounded.	R.m.D.
GLENCORSE WOOD	11th		A + B Coys in the trenches. C + D Coys in close support, employed in carrying R.E. Stores. Ammunition etc. to trenches. No casualties.	R.m.D.
GLENCORSE WOOD	12th		The Battalion was relieved at the trenches by the 9th A. + S. Highlanders, proceeded to VLAMERTINGHE for 4 days rest. No. 2309 Pte F.A. Patrick A Coy killed. 2/Lieut C.G. MELROSE + 2 other ranks wounded.	R.m.D.
VLAMERTINGHE	13th		The Battalion arrived at B Camp, VLAMERTINGHE at 5 am. Two Zeppelin bombs dropped on the Camp about 12.30 am. No damage done.	R.m.D.
VLAMERTINGHE	14th		The Battalion resting. Baths at BRANDHOEK much appreciated.	R.m.D.

R.m. Thompson Capt + adjt.
9th R. Scots

1577 Wt. W10791/1773 500,000 1/15 D. D. & L. A.D.S.S./Forms/C. 2118.

WAR DIARY

Army Form C. 2118.

Place	Date	Hour	Summary of Events and Information	Remarks and references to Appendices
VLAMERTINGHE	April 15th		Battalion resting. Battalion ordered to move to YPRES. Left VLAMERTINGHE at 8.30 p.m. & arrived YPRES 10.30 p.m. Battalion billeted in YPRES overnight.	R. in D.
YPRES	16th	8.35pm	The Battalion paraded for trenches	R. in D.
		11.45pm	Arrived GLENCORSE WOOD & relieved 9th A. & S. Highlanders. C & D Coys + M.G. Section in trenches. A + B Coys in close support. [One man slightly wounded at dumping station.]	
GLENCORSE WOOD	17th		C + D Coys + M.G. Section in trenches. [A + B Coys supplied working & carrying parties.] Sergt. W.M Black C Coy killed.	R. in D.
GLENCORSE WOOD	18th		A + B Coys relieved C + D Coys in trenches. [One man wounded.]	R. in D.
GLENCORSE WOOD	19th		A + B Coys + M.G. Section in trenches. C + D Coys supplied working & carrying parties.	R. in D.
GLENCORSE WOOD	20th		do.	R. in D.
			Sergt. L. Young killed, 2 men wounded. Transport shelled in YPRES. One man wounded.	R. in D.

WAR DIARY
or
INTELLIGENCE SUMMARY.
(Erase heading not required.)

Army Form C. 2118.

Place	Date	Hour	Summary of Events and Information	Remarks and references to Appendices
VLAMERTINGHE	1915 April 21st	12.30 a.m	The Battalion relieved at trenches by 9th A & S Highlanders & proceeded to Camp A VLAMERTINGHE arriving there at 4.30 a.m. Sergeant Major P. McLACHAN joined the Battalion.	R.n.S.
do.	22nd		Battalion resting. At 8.45 pm the Battalion ordered to move.	R.n.S.
POTIJZE	23rd	3 a.m	Arrival POTIJZE WOOD & lay there to midday.	R.n.S.
		12 noon	Battalion ordered to move with D.C.L.I. under O.C. D.C.L.I.	
		12.30 pm	A + B Coys ordered to ST. JULIEN to support Canadians. 18 N.C.O's & men wounded.	
WEILTJE ST. JULIEN		3.15 pm	C + D Coys ordered to attack with D.C.L.I. York + Lancaster Regt.	
		4.15 pm	A + B Coys recalled to take part in the attack being made by the comrades. Brigade under command of Col. Turner D.C.L.I.	
WEILTJE		5/-	A + B Coys return from ST. JULIEN + advance in support of C + D Coys.	
ST. JEAN	23rd	7.30 pm	A, B + C Coys advanced to form 2000x due NORTH of ST. JEAN + commenced digging themselves in.	R.n.S. R.n. Douglas Captain Intelligence Scout

WAR DIARY
INTELLIGENCE SUMMARY

Army Form C. 2118.

VI.

Place	Date	Hour	Summary of Events and Information	Remarks and references to Appendices
ST. JEAN	1915 April 23rd	11.30 p.m	Owing to our Right being exposed + a gap of about 600' between the composite Brigade + the Canadians, orders were received to withdraw + dig ourselves in on the ridge 1400' NORTH of ST. JEAN. The casualties during the day's operations amounted to Capt. Taylor, Bell + Green + Lieut. Richard wounded. 12 N.C.O's + men killed. 98 N.C.O's + men wounded + 10 missing.	R. m. D.
ST. JEAN	24th		A + B Coys holding the line where they had commenced to dig themselves in the previous night, C + D Coys digging Support Trenches 150 yards behind. Heavily shelled but no casualties.	R. m. D.
ST. JEAN	25th		Still holding the line mentioned above. Commenced digging Communication Trenches, putting up barbed wire entanglements. Capt. J. M. Bowie, Sergt. W. S. Millikin + Sergt. J. T. Laurie + 2nd Lieut. Connelly displayed great courage + bravery while attending to wounded. They were three times shelled out of their dressing station, but still remained looking after the wounded until eventually both Capt. J. M. Bowie + Sergt. Millikin were severely wounded. R. m. Henderson Capt & acting 9.S.P. Scots	R. m. D.

WAR DIARY
or
INTELLIGENCE SUMMARY.
(Erase heading not required.)

Army Form C. 2118.

VII

Instructions regarding War Diaries and Intelligence Summaries are contained in F. S. Regs., Part II. and the Staff Manual respectively. Title pages will be prepared in manuscript.

Place	Date	Hour	Summary of Events and Information	Remarks and references to Appendices
ST. JEAN	1915 April 25th		Casualties Capt. J.M. BOWIE & Lieut. D.A.R. HADDON wounded, one man killed + 2 other ranks wounded.	R.m.D.
ST. JEAN	26th		Still holding the ridge mentioned in 23/4/15 report.	R.m.D.
ST. JEAN	27th		Relieved by the West Kent Regt. at 2 am. proceeded to POTIJZE WOOD remained in support there during the day. At 11 p.m orders were received to proceed to SANCTUARY WOOD to form part of the Reserve of the 82nd Brigade. Lieuts. P.J. BLAIR & R.S. LINDSAY rejoined the Battalion	R.m.D.
SANCTUARY WOOD	28th		Working on subsidiary line. Casualties 1 man killed & 1 man wounded.	R.m.D.
—do—	29th		Rejoined the 81st Brigade. Provided working parties to work on subsidiary line. Casualties one man killed.	R.m.D.
—do.—	30th		Provided working parties to work on subsidiary line. Casualties one man wounded.	R.m.D. R.m. Denkynson Capt. & A/tft. gazetted 1st Lieuts

81st Inf.Bde.
27th Div.

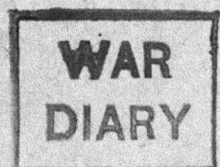

9th BATTN. THE ROYAL SCOTS.

M A Y

1 9 1 5

WAR DIARY or INTELLIGENCE SUMMARY

Army Form C. 2118.

9th Batt. (Highlanders) The Royal Scots.

Place	Date	Hour	Summary of Events and Information	Remarks and references to Appendices
HOOGE	1st May 1915		Battalion in demi repose in SANCTUARY WOOD. Provided working parties to work on subsidiary line and construction of dugouts in ZOUAVE WOOD. One man wounded.	P. h. Q.
— " —	2nd		Still in demi repose in SANCTUARY WOOD and provided working parties to work on subsidiary line. At 6 p.m. received orders to proceed to POTIJZE with 2nd Cameron Highlanders under command of Lt. Col. J. Campbell D.S.O. Arrived at POTIJZE at 7.30 p.m. and remained there until orders were received at 9.30 p.m. to return to SANCTUARY WOOD. One man wounded.	P. h. Q.
— " —	3rd		Battalion working on new line of trenches and construction of dugouts. At 4.15 p.m. received orders to proceed to VERLORENHOEK with 2nd Cameron Highlanders [under command of Lt. Col. Campbell D.S.O.] Working parties were withdrawn and the Battalion Left SANCTUARY WOOD at 5 p.m. and marched to the level crossing in J11.B. [where orders were received to occupy a line of shelter trenches in J5.D.] At 8.30 p.m. orders were received to proceed to FREZENBERG via VERLORENHOEK arriving there at 10 p.m. At 10.45 p.m. orders were received to return to SANCTUARY WOOD. Two men wounded.	P. h. Q. P. h. Bridgman Capt & adjt 9th Royal Scots

Army Form C. 2118.

WAR DIARY
or
INTELLIGENCE SUMMARY.
(Erase heading not required.)

9th Batt. (Highlanders)
The Royal Scots.

Instructions regarding War Diaries and Intelligence Summaries are contained in F. S. Regs., Part II. and the Staff Manual respectively. Title pages will be prepared in manuscript.

Place	Date	Hour	Summary of Events and Information	Remarks and references to Appendices
HOOGE	4/5/15		Took over line of trenches from 1st Argyll & Sutherland Highlanders at 9 p.m. A & B Coys in first line trenches and C & D Coys in support. One man wounded.	R. b. D.
"	5/5/15		A & B Coys in Trenches and C & D Coys in support. Work was carried out on the improvement of trenches and the construction of dug outs. One man wounded.	R. b. D.
"	6/5/15		C & D Coys took over 1st line trenches from A & B Coys at 9 p.m. One man wounded.	R. b. D.
"	7/5/15		C & D Coys in first line trenches and A & B Coys in support. Two men wounded.	R. b. D.
"	8/5/15		C & D Coys in first line trenches, A & B Coys in support. Were heavily shelled during the day. The enemy attacked the trenches on our left held by the 2nd Gloucesters, but no attack was made on the line held by my Battalion. Lieut W.S.S. LYON and two other ranks killed and nine other ranks wounded. 2/Lieuts [B.E. Yeats, A.H. Douglas, A.H. Macfarlane, and T.S.H. Lawson] and 70 other ranks joined the Battalion. [Lieut (J.J. Burns)]	R. b. D. R. b. Chargès. Cap & app. 9th Royal Scots

1577 Wt. W10791/1773 500,000 1/15 D.D.&L. A.D.S.S./Forms/C. 2118.

Army Form C. 2118.

WAR DIARY
or
INTELLIGENCE SUMMARY.

9th Batt. (Highlanders) The Royal Scots.

(Erase heading not required.)

Instructions regarding War Diaries and Intelligence Summaries are contained in F.S. Regs., Part II. and the Staff Manual respectively. Title pages will be prepared in manuscript.

Place	Date	Hour	Summary of Events and Information	Remarks and references to Appendices
HOOGE	9/5/15		A, B & C Coys in first-line trenches and D Coy in support. The enemy continued their bombardment and attacked the trenches on our immediate left. Twelve other ranks wounded.	R.W.D.
"	10/5/15		A, B & C Coys in first-line trenches and D Coy in support. The enemy continued their bombardment and made further attacks against the trenches on our immediate left. One other rank killed and two other ranks wounded. [2/Lieut. B. E. Yeats sent to Hospital suffering from shock due to shell fire.]	R.W.D.
"	11/5/15		A, B & C Coys in first-line trenches and D Coy in support. Two other ranks killed and seven other ranks wounded. 3 2/Lieuts. [G. A. Bentinck, G. M. McGregor & W. M. Morris] joined the Battalion.	R.W.D.
"	12/5/15		A, B & C Coys in first-line trenches with D Coy in support. 2/Lieut. A. H. MACFARLANE killed and four other ranks wounded.	R.W.D.

R. W. Dudgeon Capt & adjt
9th Royal Scots

Army Form C. 2118.

WAR DIARY
or
INTELLIGENCE SUMMARY.

9th Batt. (Highlanders) The Royal Scots.

IV

(Erase heading not required.)

Instructions regarding War Diaries and Intelligence Summaries are contained in F. S. Regs., Part II. and the Staff Manual respectively. Title pages will be prepared in manuscript.

Place	Date	Hour	Summary of Events and Information	Remarks and references to Appendices
HOOGE	13/5/15		A B & C Coys in first line trenches with D Coy in support. Four other ranks wounded.	R.n.D.
"	14/5/15		A B & C Coys in first line trenches. D Coy in support. D Coy relieved B Coy in first line trenches at 10 p.m. Three other ranks killed and one other ranks wounded.	R.n.D.
"	15/5/15		A C & D Coys in first line trenches & B Coy in support. One other rank killed and three other ranks wounded.	R.n.D.
"	16/5/15		A C & D Coys in first line trenches & B Coy in support. Two other ranks killed and two other ranks wounded.	R.n.D.
"	17/5/15		A C & D Coys in first line trenches & B Coy in support. One other rank killed and eight other ranks wounded.	R.n.D.
"	18/5/15		A C & D Coys in first line trenches and B Coy in support. Three other ranks wounded.	R.n.D.

R tr Duntyton Capt & adjt
9th Royal Scots

WAR DIARY
or
INTELLIGENCE SUMMARY.

Army Form C. 2118.

9th Batt. (Highlanders) The Royal Scots.

(Erase heading not required.)

Place	Date	Hour	Summary of Events and Information	Remarks and references to Appendices
	1915			
HOOGE	19/5/15		A C & D Coys in first line trenches & B Coy in support. No casualties.	R.h.9.
"	20/5/15		A C & D Coys in first line trenches & B Coy in support. Six other ranks wounded.	R.h.9.
"	21/5/15		A C & D Coys in first line trenches & B Coy in support. Officers of the K.O.Y.L.I. visited the trenches at 11 p.m. Three other ranks wounded.	R.h.9.
"	22/5/15		The Battalion was relieved by the 1st K.O.Y.L.I at 11 p.m. and marched to BUSSEBOOM, arriving there at 4 a.m. Three other ranks killed and four other ranks wounded.	R.h.9.
BUSSEBOOM	23/5/15		The Battalion resting.	R.h.9.
"	24/5/15	4.30p.m	28th Division being attacked on their mile front, Battalion ordered to "Stand to".	
		6.15p.m	Battalion ordered to proceed to Railway Crossing on YPRES-VLAMERTINGHE road via RENINGHELST & OUDERDOM. On arrival the Battalion bivouacked in field North of Railway Crossing.	R.h.9.

R.h. Henderson. Capt. & Adjt.
9th Royal Scots.

Army Form C. 2118.

WAR DIARY
or
INTELLIGENCE SUMMARY
(Erase heading not required.)

9th Batt. (Highlanders) The Royal Scots.

VI

Place	Date	Hour	Summary of Events and Information	Remarks and references to Appendices
VLAMERTINGHE	25/5/15		Battalion lying in reserve. At 9.30 a.m orders received to return to Camp D, VLAMERTINGHE. The Battalion lay there until 4 p.m when motor buses took the Battalion to BUSSEBOOM. [The Battalion bivouaced in wood there 4.30 pm The Rev. col. W.W. Beveridge posted to 51st Infantry Brigade and attached to Battalion.	R.n.D.
BUSSEBOOM	26/5/15		Battalion resting.	R.n.D.
" "	27/5/15		Battalion resting.	R.n.D.
" "	28/5/15	6 a.m	Battalion left BUSSEBOOM. Arrived at farm about 1500 yards South of DRANOUTRE at 10 a.m [marching via RENINGHELST, LOCRE and DRANOUTRE, and bivouaced there.]	R.n.D.
DRANOUTRE	29/5/15	5 a.m	Battalion left bivouac [and marching via BAILLEUL] arrived STEENWERCK 8.45 a.m G.O.C 3rd Corps took the Salute en route. Captain J. Ferguson and 2/Lieut A. Fraser visited trenches.	R.n.D.

Wm Rutzen Capt & adjt
9thBatt Royal Scots

1577 Wt. W10791/1773 500,000 1/15 D. D. & L. A.D.S.S./Forms/C. 2118.

WAR DIARY or INTELLIGENCE SUMMARY.

Army Form C. 2118.

9th Batt. (Highlanders) The Royal Scots.

VII

Place	Date	Hour	Summary of Events and Information	Remarks and references to Appendices
STEENWERCK	30/5/15	12.30 p.m.	Church Parade.	
		4.20 p.m.	Battalion left STEENWERCK and proceeded to ARMENTIERES arriving there 7 p.m.	P.m. ②
ARMENTIERES	31/5/15		Battalion resting.	
			R.m. Blenkinsop Capt. & adjt. 9th Royal Scots	

81st Inf.Bde.
27th Div.

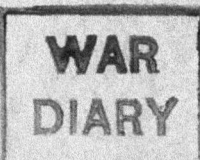

9th BATTN. THE ROYAL SCOTS.

J U N E

1 9 1 5

WAR DIARY
or
INTELLIGENCE SUMMARY.
(Erase heading not required.)

Army Form C. 2118.

9th Bn. (Highlanders)
The Royal Scots.

Place	Date	Hour	Summary of Events and Information	Remarks and references to Appendices
ARMENTIERES	1/6/15		Battalion resting.	P.m.O.
"	2/6/15		" "	
"	3/6/15		" "	P.m.O.
"	4/6/15		Lt. Col. A.S. Blair & Capt. P.M. Snodgrass visited the trenches held by the 1st Royal Scots, 2nd Gloucesters & 1st A.& S. Highlrs.	P.m.O.
"	5/6/15		Battalion resting.	
"	6/6/15		" "	P.m.O.
"	7/6/15		Battalion inspected by Major General PULTENEY Commanding 3rd Corps. Capts. P.M. Snodgrass, J. Ferguson, P.A. Blair & Lieuts. Liddle, Wardrop & Douglas visited the trenches held by 1st A.& S. Highlrs.	P.m.O. P.m. Gunnison Corps & adjt. g.a.p.w.e. Gues

WAR DIARY or INTELLIGENCE SUMMARY.

9th Bn. (Highlanders) The Royal Scots.

Army Form C. 2118.

Place	Date	Hour	Summary of Events and Information	Remarks and references to Appendices
CHAPELLE D'ARMENTIERES	8/6/15		H.Q. move to CHAPELLE D'ARMENTIERES and A + B Coys take over trenches 71 + 72 from the 1st A. + S. Highrs. C + D Coys in Reserve.	P. M. D.
"	9/6/15		A + B Coys in Trenches. C + D Coys in Reserve.	P. M. D.
"	10/6/15		"	
"	11/6/15		"	P. M. D.
"	12/6/15		"	
"	13/6/15		"	
"	14/6/15		C + D Coys in Trenches. A + B Coys in Reserve. No 2132 Pte. J. Emmett (B Coy) wounded.	P. M. D.
"	15/6/15			P. M. D. Dunkerque Cups. & adpt. Glasgow Yeor. Cs

Army Form C. 2118.

WAR DIARY
or
INTELLIGENCE SUMMARY

(Erase heading not required.)

9th Bn. (Highlanders) The Royal Scots.

Instructions regarding War Diaries and Intelligence Summaries are contained in F.S. Regs., Part II. and the Staff Manual respectively. Title pages will be prepared in manuscript.

Place	Date	Hour	Summary of Events and Information	Remarks and references to Appendices
CHAPELLE D'ARMENTIERES	16/6/15		A & D Coys in trenches. A & B Coys in Reserve. Pte W. Ross & Pte W. Mathieson went out on patrol about 11 p.m. Lieut. N. MacDonald & Lieut N. MacDonald & party of 12 taken over by 2nd Cameron Highrs. A & B Coys in Reserve. No. 1978 Pte. R.H. Gibson killed. Sergt. W.J. Laidie & Pte W. Mathieson went out on patrol & searched the ground in front of trenches 71 & 72 nightly up to the German wire entanglements but could find no trace of Lieut. N. MacDonald & Pte. W. Ross.	W.R.D.
			were entanglements while close up to the German trenches a stray shot hit Pte. W. Ross, which made him give a shout. The Germans turned search light on to the spot and opened rapid fire. Pte. Mathieson returned about 12.25 a.m. 17/6/15 stated that when rapid fire was opened on the patrol, they scattered by rolling over in the grass. He lay still for about 15 minutes, when the rapid fire ceased. He then crawled about looking for Lieut. W. MacDonald & Pte. W. Ross but could find no trace of them, or in his German Lieut. N. MacDonald is now wounded and a prisoner, & Pte W. Ross wounded & a prisoner.	
	17/6/15		C & D Coys in trenches. D. Coy take over 73 trench from the K.R.R. 71 trench & front of 72 taken over by 2nd Cameron Highrs. A & B Coys in Reserve. No. 1978 Pte. R.H. Gibson killed. Sergt. W.J. Laidie & Pte W. Mathieson went out on patrol & searched the ground in front of trenches 71 & 72 nightly up to the German wire entanglements but could find no trace of Lieut. N. MacDonald & Pte. W. Ross.	W.R.D.

P.H. Mathieson Copl & Sergt J.H. Ross a Pte.

1577 Wt. W10794/1773 500,000 1/15 D.D.&L. A.D.S.S./Forms/C. 2118.

Army Form C. 2118.

WAR DIARY
or
INTELLIGENCE SUMMARY

(Erase heading not required.)

IV

9th Bn. (Highlanders) The Royal Scots.

Instructions regarding War Diaries and Intelligence Summaries are contained in F.S. Regs., Part II. and the Staff Manual respectively. Title pages will be prepared in manuscript.

Place	Date	Hour	Summary of Events and Information	Remarks and references to Appendices
CHAPELLE D'ARMENTIERES	18/6/15		C & D Coys in the trenches. A & B Coys in Reserve.	P.m. D.
	19/6/15		" No. 1820 Pte. D. Edwards C. Coy wounded	P.S.D.
	20/6/15		A + B Coys in the trenches C + D Coys in Reserve.	P.K.C.
	21/6/15		"	
	22/6/15		"	
	23/6/15		"	12 Bn. D.
	24/6/15		"	
	25/6/15		"	

1577 Wt. W10791/1773 500,000 1/15 D. D. & L. A.D.S.S./Forms/C. 2118.

Army Form C. 2118.

WAR DIARY
or
INTELLIGENCE SUMMARY.

9th B. (Highlanders)
The Royal Scots.

(Erase heading not required.)

Instructions regarding War Diaries and Intelligence Summaries are contained in F. S. Regs., Part II and the Staff Manual respectively. Title pages will be prepared in manuscript.

Place	Date	Hour	Summary of Events and Information	Remarks and references to Appendices
CHAPELLE D'ARMENTIERES	26/6/15		A + B Coys in Trenches. C + D Coys in Reserve.	R.n.D.
"	27/6/15		A + B Coys hand over trench 73 to the Shropshire Light Infantry. C + D Coys take over trench 64 from 1st A. + S. Highlrs. Headquarters move from billets in CHAPELLE D'ARMENTIERES to "The Orchard" in I.15.6. A + B Coys in Reserve.	R.n.D.
"	28/6/15		C + D Coys in trenches. A + B Coys in Reserve	R.n.D.
"	29/6/15		" Pt. J. Seaton £ Coy wounded while attending Bomb School.	R.n.D.
"	30/6/15		C + D Coys in trenches. A + B Coys in Reserve.	R.n.D.

R.n. Kempson Capt & adjt
9th Royal Scots

81st Inf.Bde.
27th Div.

9th BATTN. THE ROYAL SCOTS.

J U L Y

1 9 1 5

9th Bn (Highland)
The Royal Scots

Army Form C. 2118.

WAR DIARY
or
INTELLIGENCE SUMMARY.
(Erase heading not required.)

Instructions regarding War Diaries and Intelligence Summaries are contained in F. S. Regs., Part II. and the Staff Manual respectively. Title pages will be prepared in manuscript.

Place	Date	Hour	Summary of Events and Information	Remarks and references to Appendices
ORCHARD RUE GATTIGNIES	1/7/15	—	"C" + "D" Coys in the trenches "A" + "B" Coys in Reserve	R.M.D.
—"—	2/7/15	—	"C" + "D" Coys in the trenches "A" + "B" Coys in Reserve 10. N.C.O.s + men sent to LA BOUDRELLE for instruction in Bomb throwing	R.M.D.
—"—	3/7/15	—	"A" + "B" Coys relieved "C" + "D" Coys in the trenches. "C" + "D" Coys in Reserve.	R.M.D.
—"—	4/7/15	—	"A" + "B" Coys in the trenches "C" + "D" Coys in Reserve. 4 N.C.O.s sent to attend a course of instruction in the use of the BARR + STROUD Range finder.	R.M.D.
—"—	5/7/15	—	"A" + "B" Coys in the trenches "C" + "D" Coys in Reserve	R.M.D.
—"—	6/7/15	—	"A" + "B" Coys in the trenches "C" + "D" Coys in Reserve	R.M.D.
—"—	7/7/15	—	"A" + "B" Coys in the trenches "C" + "D" Coys in Reserve. A draft consisting of 2 Sergts. 1 Cpl + 12 men reported for duty from No 2 Territorial Base Camp. War Loan Leaflets issued	R.M.D.

R.M. Hodgson Capt + adjt
9th Royal Scots

9th Bn (Highland)
The Royal Scots

Army Form C. 2118.

WAR DIARY
or
INTELLIGENCE SUMMARY.
(Erase heading not required.)

Instructions regarding War Diaries and Intelligence Summaries are contained in F. S. Regs., Part II. and the Staff Manual respectively. Title pages will be prepared in manuscript.

Place	Date	Hour	Summary of Events and Information	Remarks and references to Appendices
ORCHARD RUE GATTIGNIES	8/7/15	-	"A"+"B" Coys in the trenches "C"+"D" Coys in Reserve. Pte. W. L. Gilson "A" Coy wounded. Lieut. J. T. Nicholson R.A.M.C. attached to the Bn vice Lieut J. M. Jackson R.A.M.C. transferred to Indian Corps.	R.m.D.
—"—	9/7/15	-	"C"+"D" Coys relieved "A"+"B" Coys in the trenches "A"+"B" Coys to Reserve	R.m.D.
—"—	10/7/15	-	"C"+"D" Coys in the trenches "A"+"B" Coys in Reserve.	R.m.D.
—"—	11/7/15	-	"C"+"D" Coys in the trenches "A"+"B" Coys in Reserve	R.m.D.
—"—	12/7/15	-	"C"+"D" Coys in the trenches "A"+"B" Coys in Reserve. Lieuts P.J. Blair + E. S. Fiddes + ²Lieuts D. G. Kydd + J. B. Moncrieff joined from PEEBLES.	R.m.D.
—"—	13/7/15	-	"C"+"D" Coys in the trenches "A"+"B" Coys in Reserve	R.m.D.
—"—	14/7/15	-	"C"+"D" Coys in the trenches "A"+"B" in Reserve. 10.N.C.O's + men and 16 LA BOUDRELLE for instruction in Bomb throwing. R. m. Knudsen Capt. + Adjut 9th Royal Scots.	R.m.D.

1577 Wt. W10791/1773 500,000 1/15 D. D. & L.   A.D.S.S./Forms/C. 2118.

9th Bⁿ (Highland)
Lee Royal Scots.

WAR DIARY
or
INTELLIGENCE SUMMARY
(Erase heading not required.)

Army Form C. 2118.

Place	Date	Hour	Summary of Events and Information	Remarks and references to Appendices
ORCHARD RUE GATTIGNIES	15/7/15	—	"A" + "B" Coys relieved "C" + "D" Coys in the trenches. "C" + "D" Coys to Reserve. L. Cpl. Jones + P.te. J. Tait employed as instructors at Bomb School. N° 1975 P.te. J.B. Swan "B" Coy killed.	R. m. D.
—"—	16/7/15	—	"A" + "B" Coys in the trenches. "C" + "D" Coys in Reserve. 2ⁿᵈ Lieut. E.G.A. Robb sent to ST OMER to attend Machine Gun Course.	R. m. D.
—"—	17/7/15	—	"A" + "B" Coys in the trenches. "C" + "D" Coys in Reserve. 1 Cpl. + 3 men sent to the Depot at HELFAUT for duty in connection with gas.	R. m. D.
—"—	18/7/15	—	"A" + "B" Coys in the trenches. "C" + "D" Coys in Reserve.	R. m. D.
—"—	19/7/15	—	"A" + "B" Coys in the trenches. "C" + "D" Coys in Reserve.	R. m. D.
—"—	20/7/15	—	"A" + "B" Coys in the trenches. "C" + "D" Coys in Reserve. Pte. J.H. McPherson and J.S. Leishman transferred.	R. m. D.
—"—	21/7/15	—	"C" + "D" Coys relieved "A" + "B" Coys in the trenches. "A" + "B" Coys to Reserve.	R. m. D.
—"—	22/7/15	—	"C" + "D" Coys in the trenches. "A" + "B" Coys in Reserve. 2ⁿᵈ Lieut. W.R. Spens joined from PEEBLES. R.m. Knudgson Cpl. & Acpt. G. A. Royal Scots	R. m. D.

9th Cops (Highland)
The Royal Scots

WAR DIARY or INTELLIGENCE SUMMARY.

Army Form C. 2118.

IV

Place	Date	Hour	Summary of Events and Information	Remarks and references to Appendices
ORCHARD RUE GATTIGNIES	23/7/15	—	"C" + "D" Coys in the trenches. "A" + "B" Coys in Reserve. Sngt. G.S. Brown & two men went to attend Bergues Course at CROIX-DU-BAC.	R.h.D.
— " —	24/7/15	—	"C" + "D" Coys in the trenches "A" + "B" Coys in Reserve	R.h.D.
— " —	25/7/15	—	"C" + "D" Coys in the trenches. "A" + "B" Coys in Reserve	R.h.D.
— " —	26/7/15	—	"C" + "D" Coys in the trenches. "A" + "B" Coys in Reserve. Coy.S.M. J. Ferguson. Sgt. A. Ryall. Cpls W. Clark + D. Hutchison L/Cpl R. Mitchell + Ptes T. Perry B. Mitchell. 7. Mills. G. Hutton + S. Gillespie to Cadet School ST. OMER.	R.h.D.
— " —	27/7/15	—	"A" + "B" Coys relieve "C" + "D" Coys in the trenches. "C" + "D" Coys to Reserve. No 2821 Pte T.G. Wellwood "C" Coy killed.	R.h.D.
— " —	28/7/15	—	"A" + "B" Coys in the trenches "C" + "D" Coys in Reserve. Sergt. D. Sweeney "B" Coy appointed Bandmaster 27th Division + two men joined the Band of the 27th Division. 2/Lieut G.A. McGregor + 10 N.C.Os + men went to LA BOUDRELLE for instruction in Bomb throwing	R.h.D.

R.h. Dudgeon Capt. & asst.
9th R. Royal Scots

9th Bn (Highland)
The Royal Scots

WAR DIARY
or
INTELLIGENCE SUMMARY
(Erase heading not required.)

Army Form C. 2118.

Instructions regarding War Diaries and Intelligence Summaries are contained in F.S. Regs., Part II. and the Staff Manual respectively. Title pages will be prepared in manuscript.

Place	Date	Hour	Summary of Events and Information	Remarks and references to Appendices
ORCHARD RUE GATTIGNIES	29/7/15		"A" & "B" Coys in the trenches "C" & "D" Coys in Reserve	R.m.D.
— " —	30/7/15		"A" & "B" Coys in the trenches "C" & "D" Coys in Reserve	R.m.D.
— " —	31/7/15		A & B Coys in the trenches C & D Coys in Reserve, Artillery bombardment of enemies trenches & communication trenches at intervals from 6.20 p.m. to 7.80 p.m. & at 10 p.m. "A" & "B" Coys in the trenches 6.3 opened rapid fire on the enemies salient in I. 21. 6 from 6.45-45 6.57 p.m. his M. Guns Cooperated. At 10 p.m. 3 M. Guns fired at the enemy trench opposite 63 (Traversing fire) and one M. Gun at WEZ MACQUART. We suffered no casualties as the enemies reply on our part of the line was very feeble. Capt. R. H. P. Moncrieff but into an accident while out visiting & was admitted into the 3rd Northumbrian Field Ambulance.	R.m.D.

R. m. Hodgson Capt & adjt.
9th Royal Scots

81st Inf.Bde.
27th Div.

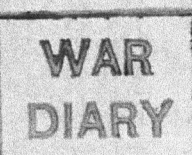

9th BATTN. THE ROYAL SCOTS.

A U G U S T

1 9 1 5

Reference Map: Belgium & France
Sheet 36 1/40,000

Army Form C. 2118.

WAR DIARY
or
INTELLIGENCE SUMMARY.
(Erase heading not required.)

9th Bn. (Highrs.) The Royal Scots.

Instructions regarding War Diaries and Intelligence Summaries are contained in F. S. Regs., Part II. and the Staff Manual respectively. Title pages will be prepared in manuscript.

Place	Date	Hour	Summary of Events and Information	Remarks and references to Appendices
THE ORCHARD RUE GATTIGNIES	1/8/15		A & B Coys in the trenches. C & D Coys in reserve. Lt. Col. Kelly gave officers of the P.P.C.L.I. visited the trenches held by A & B Coys preparatory to taking over from us on the 2nd August 1915.	R.h.D.
—	2/8/15		The P.P.C.L.I. took over the trenches held by A & B Coys at 9.30 p.m. The Battalion proceeded to a rest camp at PETIT MOULIN near ERQUINGHEM. C & D Coys arrived there at 5 p.m. & A & B Coys about 12 midnight.	R.h.D.
ERQUINGHEM	3/8/15 to 16/8/15		From the 3rd to 16th August the Battalion was at rest. Classes of Instruction for N.C.O.'s Signallers & Grenadiers were formed and a lot of useful instruction was carried out. During the period 3rd to 16th August Coys underwent the following training daily. Physical Training, one hour; Platoon & Coy close order drill, one hour; Platoon & Coy extended order drill; the remainder of the day being spent in recreation viz: swimming & football. On the 10th August General Sir Douglas Haig K.C.B., Commanding 1st Army visited the Battalion & after a time of inspection during which he spoke to the officers of the Battalion, were introduced to him, he expressed himself satisfied with all he had seen. On the 11th August Regimental Sports were held and a large number of events, mostly handicaps, with big entries were carried out. By kind permission of the G.O.C. 27th Division the Divisional Band played during the afternoon. The novelty was much appreciated by all ranks. On the 16th August the Battalion was inspected by Lieut. General Sir W.P. Pulteney, K.C.B., D.S.O., Commanding 3rd Army Corps. The Battalion was formed up in mass and the General walked round the ranks. On completion of his inspection he	R.h.D.

R.h.D. Dempson Capt. & Adjt. 9th Royal Scots

Reference Map Belgium & France II.
Sheet 36 1/20,000   9th Bn. (High'rs) The Royal Scots.

C. 2118.   Army For C. 2118.

WAR DIARY
or
INTELLIGENCE SUMMARY.
(Erase heading not required.)

Instructions regarding War Diaries and Intelligence Summaries are contained in F. S. Regs., Part II. and the Staff Manual respectively. Title pages will be prepared in manuscript.

Place	Date	Hour	Summary of Events and Information	Remarks and references to Appendices
ERQUINGHEM	16/8/15 (cont)		exerted himself satisfied with the appearance of the Battalion & complimented the Commanding Officer on the good behaviour of the Battalion, the fact being that there had not been a single Court Martial during the six months the Battalion had been on service. During the period 8th to 15th August the Battalion furnished working parties at BOIS GRENIER.	R.h.D.
LA VESÉE	16/8/15	6 & 7 Coys, Mach gun section & left half Grenadier Coy took over trench 54 from the 1st Cambridgeshire Regt. ← A & B Coys went into billets in RUE DELPIERRE.		R.h.D.
"	17/8/15	Quiet day, situation normal. Very little firing done by the enemy.		R.h.D.
"	18/8/15	Enemy sent four shells over the night of our trench about 3 p.m. No damage done. Enemy's rifle fire active between 10.30 p.m. & 12 midnight.		R.h.D.
"	19/8/15	Hostile fire during the night normal. Very few flares sent up by the enemy, & those sent up actually failed to ignite. Patrol under Lieut. E.S. Fiddes located enemy's working party & the 96th Battery opened fire on it.		R.h.D.
"	20/8/15	Situation normal. About 7 p.m. a British aeroplane was chased by a German aeroplane. The German one retired under heavy fire from our guns & dropped white lights behind the enemy's lines. A German working party was heard to our right front & rapid fire was opened on it. The working party ceased work, but it is not known whether the enemy had any casualties or not.		R.h.D.
"	21/8/15	Increase of amount of rifle fire during the night, including a considerable number of shots which seemed to come from a long range. #1246 W.A.C. Michael & Boy wounded.		R.h.D.

2353 Wt. W2544/1454 700,000 5/15 D.D.& L. A.D.S.S./Forms/C. 2118.

III.

Ref: Maps. Belgium & France
Sheet 36. N.W. 1/40,000.

Army Form C. 2118.

9th B. (Highrs) the Royal Scots.

WAR DIARY
or
INTELLIGENCE SUMMARY

(Erase heading not required.)

Instructions regarding War Diaries and Intelligence
Summaries are contained in F. S. Regs., Part II.
and the Staff Manual respectively. Title pages
will be prepared in manuscript.

Place	Date	Hour	Summary of Events and Information	Remarks and references to Appendices
LA VESEE	22/8/15		Enemy's rifle fire exceptionally little during the night. A German sniper was located and fired at by one of our snipers, & is thought the German sniper was killed. A German sniping post was detected in a tree, machine gun fire was directed against the tree at 11.30 p.m. A bombing party went out about midnight & fired eight rifle grenades at the German trench opposite.	R. n. D.
"	23/8/15		Enemy's rifle fire active during the night. Hostile aeroplane appeared over our trench at 6.20 p.m. was driven off by M.G. gun fire. Pt. L.H. Foster 2 Coy wounded.	R. n. D.
"	24/8/15		Situation normal. A & B Coys night half Rally grenadier Coy relieved C & D Coys + Left half grenadier Coy in trench 54. A & B Coy & Right half grenadier Coy went into billets in RUE DELPIERRE. Hopl. J. E. Stewart A Coy wounded.	R. n. D.
"	25/8/15		Situation normal. From reports received from a patrol sent out during the night, the German listening post at the knee of a tree at I.26.e.2.6 consists of 7 men.	R. n. D.
"	26/8/15		Enemy's rifle fire very little during the night. A German sniper was located & put out of action by one of our snipers. Enemy shelled trench 55 occupied by the 1st Royal Scots about 10.30 a.m. Our artillery (96th Battery, R.F.A.) fired at the enemy's trench opposite 54 trench, target fixed rifles. Rapell's rifles destroyed some German rifles & believed to have been killed. The Germans were observed waving flags about 1. & 5 p.m.	R. n. D.
"	27/8/15		A German working party was located & dispersed by machine gun fire. Two German aeroplanes were seen between 5.30 p.m. & 6.30 p.m. A German sniper was Killed by one of our snipers. He was dressed in a light blue uniform.	R. n. D.

R. n. Dungoon Capt & adjt
9th Royal Scots

2353 Wt. W2341/1454 700,000 5/15 D. D. & L. A.D.S.S./Forms/C. 2118.

Reference Map. Belgium & France
Sheet 36 1/40,000

WAR DIARY
or
INTELLIGENCE SUMMARY.

Army Form C. 2118.

4th Bn. (Highld.) the Royal Scots

IV

(Erase heading not required.)

Place	Date	Hour	Summary of Events and Information	Remarks and references to Appendices
LA VESÉE	28/8/15		Very quiet during the night. Enemy snipers active in the early morning. Sergt. J. Ford B Coy killed by enemy sniper about 5.30 a.m.	R. n. D.
"	29/8/15		Situation normal. A dummy was erected at the place where Sergt. Ford was killed. Own snipers kept a careful lookout. The result being that the enemy sniper was located and fired at. The sniping from that spot ceased.	R. n. D.
"	30/8/15		A German sniper was killed by one of our snipers at a point I.26.d.5.7. He was one of a working party carrying planks of wood. During the last two days the Germans have done a considerable amount of work at this point.	R. n. D.
"	31/8/15		General situation normal. During the night enemy's rifle fire exceptionally small.	R. n. D.

R. n. Anderson Capt & acting
Lieut Colonel Scots

81st Inf.Bde.
27th Div.

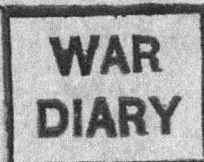

9th BATTN. THE ROYAL SCOTS.

S E P T E M B E R

1 9 1 5

9th Bn (Highland)
The Royal Scots

Reference map Belgium & France Army Form C. 2118.
Sheet 36 1/40,000

WAR DIARY
or
INTELLIGENCE SUMMARY
(Erase heading not required.)

Instructions regarding War Diaries and Intelligence Summaries are contained in F. S. Regs., Part II. and the Staff Manual respectively. Title pages will be prepared in manuscript.

Place	Date	Hour	Summary of Events and Information	Remarks and references to Appendices
LA VESÉE	1/9/15		General situation normal. Rapid fire was opened on a German working party about 11 p.m. results not known, and the Germans ceased work. "C" & "D" Coys relieved "A" & "B" Coys in the trenches. A & B Coys to billets in RUE DELPIERRE	R.n.B.
—"—	2/9/15		The Germans shelled our trench about 2.15 p.m. but no damage was done. The Germans sent up three green flares at 8.30 p.m. and another three at 9 p.m. at 9.30 p.m. the Germans swept our parapet with machine gun fire but did no damage.	R.n.B.
—"—	3/9/15		The Germans shelled our trenches between 5 p.m. & 6.30 p.m. their shooting seemed to be most erratic & their fire was apparently not aimed at a definite target. No damage was done. Pte G.H. Tait "D" Coy wounded.	R.n.B.
—"—	4/9/15		The Germans had several parties working on their trenches during the day, which were dispersed by rifle & M.G. fire. German transport was heard at 8.15 p.m. near LE QUESME FARM, rifle & artillery fire was directed on it. Lt Col. G.A. Valentine "D" Coy wounded	R.n.B. 2/Lt. Kerbyson Capt & adjt 9th Bn (Highlands) The Royal Scots

1577 Wt.W10791/1773 500,000 1/15 D.D. & L. A.D.S.S./Forms/C. 2118.

Army Form C. 2118.

WAR DIARY
or
INTELLIGENCE SUMMARY.

(Erase heading not required.)

2nd Bn (Regulars)
The Royal Scots

Instructions regarding War Diaries and Intelligence Summaries are contained in F.S. Regs., Part II. and the Staff Manual respectively. Title pages will be prepared in manuscript.

Reference map Belgium & France
Sheet 36 1/40,000

II

Place	Date	Hour	Summary of Events and Information	Remarks and references to Appendices
LA VESÉE	5/9/15		A German Aeroplane passed over our trenches about 11 a.m. & was fired at by our own anti-aircraft guns which burst it rather. About 1.30 p.m. the Germans opened h.g. fire on one of our Aeroplanes & were promptly shelled by our artillery. The German h.g. fire ceased immediately. At 5.30 p.m. a German working party was observed & was immediately fired on, the party ceased work.	R.m.B.
LA VESÉE	6/9/15		The Germans shelled our trenches about 10 a.m. No damage done. A good deal of sniping took place on both sides during the day, but the advantage was on our side. A German patrol was seen at 11.30 p.m. & rapid fire was directed on it.	R.m.B.
" "	7/9/15		A very quiet day. Nothing special to mention	R.m.B.

R.M. Rudgren Capt & Adjt
2nd Bn (Highrs)
The Royal Scots

9th Bn (Kitchener's) The Royal Scots

WAR DIARY
or
INTELLIGENCE SUMMARY

Army Form C. 2118.

Reference map Belgium & France
Sheet 36 1/40,000

Place	Date	Hour	Summary of Events and Information	Remarks and references to Appendices
LA VESÉE	8/9/15		The Germans shelled our trenches about 10 a.m. & at 3.30 p.m. No damage was done. "A" & "B" Coys relieved "C" & "D" Coys in the trenches. "C" & "D" Coys proceeded to billets in RUE DELPIERRE.	P.h.D.
—"—	9/9/15		The Germans shelled our trenches about 10.30 a.m. One shell burst on the top of a dug-out in which three men were lying. The roof of the dug-out was penetrated but the men escaped injury. Cpl G.A. Gibb "A" Coy wounded	P.h.D.
—"—	10/9/15		A German working party was heard about 10.30 p.m. They appeared to be driving in stakes. A patrol was sent out & the German working party was located. Rapid fire was directed on the German working party & they ceased work.	P.h.D.
—"—	11/9/15		The Germans shelled our trenches about 3.30 p.m. No damage was done. At 10 p.m. the Germans sent up a green rocket & opened rapid fire on our trenches for three minutes. Patrols were sent out & reported all quiet.	P.h.D.

P.h. Hodgson Capt. & adjt
9th Bn (Kitchener's) The Royal Scots

2nd Bn (Regular) The Royal Scots

Army Form C. 2118.

WAR DIARY
or
INTELLIGENCE SUMMARY
(Erase heading not required.)

Reference maps Belgium & France
S-shet 36 1/40,000
IV

Place	Date	Hour	Summary of Events and Information	Remarks and references to Appendices
LA VESÉE	12/9/15		A very quiet day. Nothing special to mention	R. M. B.
-,,-	13/9/15		The Germans shelled our trenches at 5.15 a.m. & at 10.30 a.m. No damage was done. At 3.30 p.m. our guns opened fire in the German trenches which gave off large quantities of smoke. At about 6 p.m. our guns set a farm on fire behind the German lines.	R. M. B.
-,,-	14/9/15		A very quiet day. Nothing special to mention.	R. M. B.
-,,-	15/9/15		The Battalion was relieved by the 10th Bn K. Riding Regiment about 8.30 p.m. & marched to Billets at PETIT MOULIN near ERQUINGHEM arriving there about 11 p.m.	R. M. B.

R. M. Dundgson Capt & ault
g r G Br (Hrg ldo) 2nd Royal Scots

Army Form C. 2118.

WAR DIARY
or
INTELLIGENCE SUMMARY.
(Erase heading not required.)

Army: (Regular) The Royal Scots
Reference map Belgium + France Sheet 86 1/40,000 + HAZEBROUCK Sheet 5.A 1/100000

Place	Date	Hour	Summary of Events and Information	Remarks and references to Appendices
ERQUINGHEM	16/9/15		The Battalion at Rest in Huts at PETIT MOULIN FARM.	W.m.B.
"	17/9/15		The Battalion paraded at 5 a.m. & marched to VIEUX BERQUIN arriving there at 9 a.m. (11½ miles march).	W.m.B.
VIEUX BERQUIN	18/9/15		The Battalion at Rest in Billets. The Battalion was inspected by Lieut General Sir W. P. Pulteney, K.C.B. D.S.O Commanding the 3rd Army Corps, who in his farewell address to the Battalion on leaving this Command, thanked all ranks for their loyal support & for the good work they have done.	W.m.B.
"	19/9/15		The Battalion at rest.	

Mr Anderson Capt & adgt.
g.F.Bar(Regiment)
The Royal Scots

Gordon (Highlanders)
The Royal Scots

Reference maps
HAZEBROUCK Sheet 5A 1/100,000
AMIENS Sheet 12 1/80,000

Army Form C. 2118.

WAR DIARY
or
INTELLIGENCE SUMMARY
(Erase heading not required.)

Place	Date	Hour	Summary of Events and Information	Remarks and references to Appendices
VIEUX BERQUIN	26/9/15		The Battalion paraded at 12.15 a.m. + marched to HAZEBROUCK arriving there at 4 a.m. (9 mile march). The Battalion were entrained by 5.30 a.m. & the train left at 6 a.m. The train stopped for 40 minutes at ABBEVILLE where the men had dinner. We arrived at GUILLAUCOURT at 4.15 P.M. & the Battalion was detrained & ready to march at 5 P.M. from GUILLAUCOURT and marched to our New Billeting area at LAMOTTE-EN-SANTERRE, arriving there at 6.15 P.M. (4 mile march), + took over billets from the French.	R.M.D.
LAMOTTE EN SANTERRE	29/9/15 to 30/9/15		The Battalion is in rest at LAMOTTE EN SANTERRE. During this period the Battalion were under went the following training. (1) Coy Close order + extended order drill (2) Coy in the attack (3) Battalion in the attack (4) Attack in Grenades (5) Outposts (6) Route marching	R.M.D.

R.M. Dunbarton, Capt + adjt
9th Royal Scots

81st Inf.Bde.
27th Div.

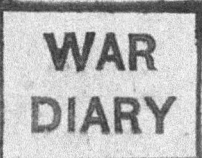

9th BATTN. THE ROYAL SCOTS.

O C T O B E R

1 9 1 5

Reference map
AMIENS Sheet 1/80,000

Gézaincourt (Chignes)
The Royal Sussex Regt. Army Form C. 2118.
I

WAR DIARY
or
INTELLIGENCE SUMMARY
(Erase heading not required.)

Instructions regarding War Diaries and Intelligence Summaries are contained in F.S. Regs., Part II. and the Staff Manual respectively. Title pages will be prepared in manuscript.

Place	Date	Hour	Summary of Events and Information	Remarks and references to Appendices
LAMOTTE EN SANTERRE	1.10.15 to 3.10.15		The Battalion in rest at LAMOTTE EN SANTERRE. During this period the Battalion underwent the following training:— (1) Coy Close order & extended order drill (2) Coy in the attack (3) Battalion in the attack (4) Route marches.	R.H.D.
FONTAINE LES CAPPY	4.10.15		The Battalion paraded at 6.45 P.M. & marched to CHIGNES & FONTAINE LES CAPPY arriving at CHIGNES at 11.30 A.M. where A & B Coys were billeted & at the CHATEAU FONTAINE LES CAPPY at 12 NOON (12½ mile march) & relieved the 1/2nd CAMBRIDGESHIRE Regt.	R.H.D.
FONTAINE LES CAPPY	5.10.15 to 24.10.15		During this period the Battalion found the Scene Reserve for the 8/9th Infy Brigade & were employed in mining operations under the supervision of the 2nd WESSEX FIELD COY R.E. A draft consisting of 106 N.C.O's & men arrived from England at 8. P.M. on 20/10/15.	R.H.D.
FONTAINE LES CAPPY	24.10.15		The Battalion was relieved at the CHATEAU FONTAINE LES CAPPY & CHIGNES by the 5th Regt d'Infne at 4 P.M. & marched to Billets at LAMOTTE EN SANTERRE arriving there at 8.15 P.M. (12½ mile march) R.H. Hudgson Capt. & Adjt. 9th Royal Sussex	R.H.D.

Reference maps
AMIENS & MONTDIDIER Sheets 1/80,000

9 Coys (Rifles)
1st Royal Scots

WAR DIARY or **INTELLIGENCE SUMMARY**
(Erase heading not required.)

Army Form C. 2118.

II

Instructions regarding War Diaries and Intelligence Summaries are contained in F. S. Regs., Part II and the Staff Manual respectively. Title pages will be prepared in manuscript.

Place	Date	Hour	Summary of Events and Information	Remarks and references to Appendices
LAMOTTE EN SANTERRE	25/10/15		The Battalion resting	P.M.D.
LAMOTTE EN SANTERRE	26/10/15		The Battalion paraded at 8.A.M & marched to BOVES arriving there at 12.30.p.m. (12 mile march). The Battalion spent the night 26th/27th under Canvas.	P.M.D.
BOVES	27/10/15		The Battalion paraded at 7.A.M & marched to BOUGAINVILLE (18 mile march). A halt of 1½ hours was made at PISSY where the men had their dinners. The Battalion arrived at BOUGAINVILLE at 2.30.P.M.	P.M.D.
BOUGAINVILLE	28/10/15 to 31/10/15		During this period this Corps went for route marches daily, & all ranks were practised in throwing grenades. Courses of instruction for the training of Reserve machine gunners & signallers were formed	P.M.D. P.M. Lindsey Capt & adjt 1st Royal Scots

2353 Wt. W2544/1454 700,000 5/15 D. D. & L. A.D.S.S./Forms/C. 2118.

81st Bde.
27th Div.

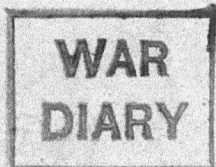

Left to join 5th Division 24th Nov.1915.

9th ROYAL SCOTS

NOVEMBER

1 9 1 5

Reference Map:
AMIENS Sheet 12 1/80,000
Army Form C. 2118.
Sheet 7.

WAR DIARY or INTELLIGENCE SUMMARY.

9th Battn. (Highlanders)
The Royal Scots.

Instructions regarding War Diaries and Intelligence Summaries are contained in F. S. Regs. Part II. and the Staff Manual respectively. Title pages will be prepared in manuscript.

(Erase heading not required.)

Place	Date	Hour	Summary of Events and Information	Remarks and references to Appendices
BOUGAINVILLE	1/11/15 to 9/11/15		The Battalion resting in BOUGAINVILLE. During this period Coys went route marches daily, and all ranks were instructed in the use of grenades. A Machine Gun Course of Instruction was carried out and a Machine Gun Reserve formed. Courses of Instruction in Bugling, semaphore & morse signalling and lamp & helio signalling were carried out.	R. In. B.
	10/11/15		Major-General G. F. Milne, C.B., D.S.O. made a farewell address to the Officers of the Battalion & expressed his satisfaction at what the Battalion had done in the past, and his great regret that he was not able to have us still under his command when the Division went to Serbia.	R. In. B.
	11/11/15 to 27/11/15		At 12 noon Brigadier General H. L. Croker, C.B., commanding 81st Infantry Brigade inspected the Battalion and made a farewell speech in which he complimented the Battalion on their appearance and high state of efficiency. During this period the Machine Gun and Signalling Courses of Instruction and the Course of Instruction in the use of Grenades were continued and completed. The Coys also went route marches daily.	R. In. B.

R. In. Henderson Capt. + adjt.
9th Royal Scots.

Reference Maps:
AMIENS Sheet 12 1/5,000.
France Sheet 62d N.E. 1/20,000
        62d N.W. 1/5,000.

Instructions regarding War Diaries and Intelligence Summaries are contained in F.S. Regs., Part II. and the Staff Manual respectively. Title pages will be prepared in manuscript.

WAR DIARY or INTELLIGENCE SUMMARY.

9th Battalion (Highlanders) The Royal Scots.

Army Form C. 2118.

Sheet IV.

(Erase heading not required.)

Place	Date	Hour	Summary of Events and Information	Remarks and references to Appendices
BOUGAINVILLE	23/11/15		The Battalion left BOUGAINVILLE at 2 p.m. and marched to FERRIERES (7 miles) where it billeted for the night.	P.m.B.
FERRIERES	24/11/15		The Battalion moved from FERRIERES at 9 a.m. and marched to PONT NOYELLES (13 miles) where it billeted for the night. Major General G.F. Milne, C.B., D.S.O, Commanding 27th Division took the salute as the Battalion marched past at FERRIERES. He handed to the Commanding Officer a farewell message in which he desired to express to all ranks his appreciation of the high state of efficiency of the Battalion and of their splendid behaviour during the time they had been in the 27th Division, and, that they had worthily maintained the character of their race, and he wished them goodbye with the greatest regret. The Battalion came under the orders of the G.O.C. 5th Division at PONT NOYELLES.	P.m.B.
PONT NOYELLES	25/11/15		The Battalion paraded at 9 a.m. marched to SAILLY LORETTE where it billeted for the night. (10 miles).	P.m.B.
SAILLY LORETTE	26/11/15		The Battalion paraded at 9.30 a.m. marched to SUZANNE (11 miles), and joined the 14th Infantry Brigade there. A.C of marched on to VAUX, where they were instructed in patrol work etc. by the 1/5th Cheshire Regt. preparatory to the Battalion taking over.	P.m.B.

R. W. Sandeman Capt. & Adjt.
9th Royal Scots.

Reference Map.
FRANCE Sheet 62c NW 1/20000

9th Bn (Argyllshire)
The Royal Scots

Army Form C. 2118.

Sheet III

WAR DIARY
or
INTELLIGENCE SUMMARY.
(Erase heading not required.)

Instructions regarding War Diaries and Intelligence Summaries are contained in F.S. Regs., Part II. and the Staff Manual respectively. Title pages will be prepared in manuscript.

Place	Date	Hour	Summary of Events and Information	Remarks and references to Appendices
SUZANNE	27/11/15	6.28 11/15	B. C. & D. Companies in SUZANNE. A draft consisting of 19 other ranks joined the Battalion from ENGLAND	P.m.S.
VAUX	28/11/15	6.28 11/15	A Coy at VAUX being instructed by 1/5th Cheshires in patrol work on the marshes	P.m.S.
SUZANNE	29/11/15		B. C. & D. Coys paraded at 7 a.m. & relieved the 1/5th Cheshires at Bois de VAUX (C coy) ROYAL DRAGONS WOOD (D coy) ½ Coy in RESERVE at VAUX ½ Bcoy at NEW SHELTERS & ½ Bcoy D coy 1/5th Cheshires A coy took over Charge of VAUX from D coy Battalion H.Q. moved to VAUX	P.m.S.
VAUX	30/11/15		A quiet day. Patrols on the marshes at night came into contact with German patrols.	P.m.S.

P.M. Sturgeon Capt & Adjt
9th Royal Scots

g/R. Scott
Intell Report
Nov 1915

Army Form C. 2118.

WAR DIARY
or
INTELLIGENCE SUMMARY.
(Erase heading not required.)

Instructions regarding War Diaries and Intelligence Summaries are contained in F. S. Regs., Part II. and the Staff Manual respectively. Title pages will be prepared in manuscript.

Place	Date	Hour	Summary of Events and Information	Remarks and references to Appendices
Vaux	29.XI.15		Patrol of 5th CHES. REGT under 2nd Lt F BISHOP, 5th CHES. REGT, accompanied by Scout Officers of 9th ROYAL SCOTS proceeded to Karal at 9.30 A.M. All ground in vicinity of wood (5c) was examined but no tracks found. Patrol then proceeded through wood (5a, 5b) towards (CUREU). Small Patrols examined land & demolished shews at FARGNY CAUSEWAY (5b) & also line of poplars (6a, 6c) starting from West end of Wood (5-6). Both patrols reported nil. Patrol returned 12 Noon. No other observation possible owing to weather.	FRANCE ("B" Series) SHEET 62° N.W. $\frac{1}{20,000}$

R. Lindsay
Capt. 9th Royal Scots
29.XI.15 – 3.45 P.M.

WAR DIARY or INTELLIGENCE SUMMARY

(Erase heading not required.)

Army Form C. 2118.

Place	Date	Hour	Summary of Events and Information	Remarks and references to Appendices
VAUX	29.XI.15		At 2.30 P.M. Sent Officers of 9th Royal Scots and 5th Ches. Regt. proceeded to Reconnoitre and examined the FAUSE when they entertained O.C. Faust left 20 German patrols had been noted at FAUSE. Patrol returned at 5 P.M. Nil Report. At 6.15 P.M. Officers patrol proceeded to Reconnoitre, trying to obtain sketching near patrol remained on CAUSEWAY (S.E.). A small patrol was pushed out towards CAUSE Abbey wood (S.E.), worked up on a Southerly direction. It returned by FAUSE path Whole patrol returned at 10 P.M. Nothing to report.	FRANCE ("B" Series) SHEET 62⁰ N.W. 1/20,000
VAUX	30.XI.15		Patrol of 9th Royal Scots and 5th Ches. Regt. started at 9.45 A.M. with object of finding whether enemy had approached posts on CAUSEWAY (S.E.) during night of 29th/30th. Patrol went on the lookes from heads of CAUSEWAY & examined ground between West end of wood (S.E.) & West end of wood (S.E.) through glasses. Patrol returned at 12.15 Noon, reported nothing.	

R. Kinchan
Capt. 9th Royal Scots
30.XI.15
4. O.P.2.

5th Division

14th Bde.

9th Royal Scots

Came from 27 Div. Nov. 24-15.

December 1915

14th Bde.
5th Div.

Came from 27th Division 24th November 1915.

9th ROYAL SCOTS.

DECEMBER

1 9 1 5

Reference Map
FRANCE Sheet 62 C. N.W.

Army Form C. 2118.

9th Bn (Highld)
The Royal Scots
I

WAR DIARY
INTELLIGENCE SUMMARY
(Erase heading not required.)

Place	Date	Hour	Summary of Events and Information	Remarks and references to Appendices
VAUX	1/12/15 to 11/12/15		The Battalion occupied sub-sector A.1, which is composed of the defences of VAUX, BOIS de VAUX and ROYAL DRAGONS WOOD. The scouts patrolled the marsh daily, day & night but did not come in contact with a German patrol. Coys were busily employed in repairing trenches, communication trenches & in erection of screens.	AAB
VAUX	12th to 16th		The Battalion less B.Coy & 1 Platoon C.Coy occupied sub-sector A.1. as above. B.Coy & 1 Platoon C.Coy relieved 1 Coy. D.C.L.I. in trenches 10, 11, &12 at MOULIN de FARGNY. The Scouts patrolled the marsh & carefully reconnoitred LA GRENOUILLERE – a pot-hill by the Germans, with a view to bombing it. They got close up to the German trench without being observed. On the 16th No 1509 Pte T.G. MYLES was killed in action while attached to the West Bomb Thrower Section.	AAB
VAUX	17th to 27th		The Battalion occupied sub-sector A.1. as above. The Scouts patrolled the marsh day & night, but did not come in contact with German patrols. A draft consisting of 79 men O.R. joined the Battalion from England on the 18th.	ASB

A Blair Lt Col

Reference Map.
FRANCE
Sheet 62.c. N.W.

Army Form C. 2118.

9th Bn (H'rs)
The Royal Scots
II

WAR DIARY
INTELLIGENCE SUMMARY
(Erase heading not required.)

Place	Date	Hour	Summary of Events and Information	Remarks and references to Appendices
VAUX.	28th		One squadron NORTH HANTS Yeomanry relieved D. Coy in ROYAL DRAGON'S WOOD. On relief II. Coy marched to VAUX. B. Coy & 1 platoon C. Coy took over trenches 10, 11 & 12 at MOULIN de FARGNY from C. Coy. 2d MANCHESTERS. A. Coy at VAUX, 3 platoons C. Coy at VAUX WOOD. The Scouts patrolled the marsh day & night.	all
VAUX	29th		A & D Coys at VAUX. 3 platoons C. Coy at VAUX WOOD & B. Coy & 1 platoon C. Coy at MOULIN de FARGNY. The Scouts patrolled the marsh as usual.	all
VAUX.	30th		D. Coy & 1 platoon C. Coy relieved B. Coy & 1 platoon C. Coy at MOULIN de FARGNY. On relief II Coy proceeded to VAUX. A & D. Coys at VAUX. 3 platoons C. Coy at VAUX WOOD. No 3246 Pte J. S. ROBERTS was killed in action at MOULIN de FARGNY. The Scouts patrolled the marsh as usual.	all
VAUX.	31st		A & B. Coy at VAUX. 3 platoons C. Coy at VAUX WOOD. D. Coy & 1 platoon C. Coy at MOULIN de FARGNY. The Scouts patrolled the marsh as usual. During the period 1/7/15 to 31/7/15 the weather was very broken and a lot of work was done in the repair & drainage of fire communication trenches. The health of the Battalion was satisfactory & the moral good.	all

A. S. Blair Lt Col